Dragonfly Messages

A Poetry Collection

Kym Sheehan

BookLeaf
Publishing
India | USA | UK

Made with ❤ on the BookLeaf Publishing Platform
www.bookleafpub.in
www.bookleafpub.com

Dedication

For my girls, Lissa and Carrie, who made me stronger,
and their families; all of whom are my heart and soul.

Preface

"Wring is easy. All you have to do is sit down at the
typewriter, cut open a vein, and bleed."
Red Sith, sportswriter

Writing is in my blood. Since I was able to hold a crayon,
I loved to write and create art with words and pictures.
This passion developed from a love of reading. My work
with the National Writing Project, specifically, The
Tampa Bay Writing Project, help to begin my adulthood
journey of writing. Poetry keeps us honest with word
choice and brevity. It is my hope you take something
away after reading, and that you can see yourself within
the words. There may be a specific meaning for me, but
remember, do not look for my meaning, look inside
yourself and find meaning that makes sense to you.
Thanks for taking the time to read.

Acknowledgements

First and foremost, I want to acknowledge my family and
friends, all of whom encourage me to be me. Many
thanks to the students and teachers that I have written
with over the last 30 years, who taught me as much as I
hope I taught them. If not for the multitude of writing
workshops I taught and/or attended, I would not have
the courage to publish my personal writings. To my
fellow writers in the Tampa Bay Writing Project, I wish
to recognize each person for their unending support over
the years, and the friendships that came from our
sharing of words. Finally, I want to thank Book Leaf
Publishing for this opportunity.

1. Dragonfly

Dragonfly

Each time my life feels broken or
I need to pause and reflect,
one or more dragonflies
appear and a calm envelope me.

This totem represents new beginnings,
Hope, good luck, and transformation.

I love dragonflies! And they love me.

In the end, dragonflies are the
Messengers, they are my totems and my muses.
When you see one,
It's me; watching over you,
Forever and always.

Author's note: Dragonflies are my totem. They visit me when I need them. Appearing as prehistoric insects, they are the messengers of past, present, and future. Dragonflies represent transformation and change, joys and sorrows, and strength and courage. Dragonflies represent me.

2. To My Muse - The Dragonfly

To My Muse - The Dragonfly

You visit me in spurts of time,
sometimes staying for an hour or a day,
sometimes for a month or two.
I need you to soothe the savage critic within me.
You allow me to write with reckless literary abandum.

You travel beside me as I journey back in time,
Into the future, or you simply be and allow me to be
present.
We spread our wings and fly.
Your steadfast presence pushes me to order my thoughts,
and emotions to provide clarity to each piece of writing.

My muse - we are messengers.
I am you and you are me,
Together we are one and whole,
writing with passion and delight.

Dragonfly Message: Everyone has a muse, find yours and
let the muse guide
you where you need to go.

3. Rise Up and Be Strong

Rise Up and Be Strong!

The sun weaves its way through the bedroom blinds.
It's early, I stir awake, and I am grateful for another day.
I lift my legs toward the sky,
aiming to stretch before rising.

I gaze upon my once supple legs and
begin to laugh aloud.
My legs resemble drooping fabric that look like
the swirling bark of a banyan tree,
with its gnarly branches that
seem to ripple when swaying in the breeze.
Like the tree, my legs are
representative of long-life.
I laugh again.

Some see wrinkles and scars

nothing except wear and tear
of an aging body.
While that may be partially
true, I view this aging as
a personal strength,
and being rooted in the earth.
I embrace each defect I possess,
because they are my strength
and my story.

I have learned that our outer trappings,
the grey hair, wrinkles and scars,
tell a story that no one else
knows in its totality.
I carry myself with pride,
knowing I've done my best.
The markings I bear, like that of a banyan tree ,
depict my story, at least
part of the journey.

Those deep lines, and faded scars
represent my search for 'the grail',
whatever it may be.
I stand rooted in this world,
and possess a simple wisdom of life.

My branches are strongly
rooted in family and friends,
and often indistinguishable from,
and entangled with one another.
My prosperity is family and friends, not coins.
I am rich beyond means.

Like the tree, I wish to symbolize life,
growth, and a bit of wisdom.
Trees continue to dance between life and death,
each swaying limb reaches out,
protecting, and sometimes breaking.
I too, will raise my limbs toward the sky
and be thankful for the day ahead.
All this... from a simple stretch.

Dragonfly Message: We all possess an inner strength
which
we sometimes choose to hide.
Be you, dig deep, and use the power within you.
You may surprise yourself.

4. A Snapshot Look: Grandma Dot

A Snapshot Look:
Grandma Dot

Fragile spindles lay at rest after years of toil.
I miss the snapshot look of
right hand atop the left.
The yellowed, wrinkled mass, lined with a map of
blue veins became one.
Her hands neatly trimmed,
but there is no manicure here.
Each scar, groove and fold of skin represents
a life of demanding work.
Her brittle hands rest upon the blue, crocheted blanket,
that shrouds her knees.

Mostly, the hands lay motionless.
A twitch here, a slight movement there,

Those long, slender fingers lost their strength long ago.
Gone too is the skin's elasticity, and
Like the blanket, the skin drapes across its subject –
those brittle hands...oh, so cold.
Cold hands – warm heart.

Movement of her hands toward the teacup is a maneuver
in slow-motion.
The clinking cup sounds against the saucer,
and highlights her lack of control.
Drops of tannic acid dot a trail from table to lap.
The cup shakes as if the earth were moving.
Another set of clinking sounds and trembling
movements
signal the end of activity.
The yellowed, wrinkled mass returns to stillness.

Dragonfly Message: Years of toil affect most people, yet
the elderly seem to lack acknowledgement of their life's
accomplishments. They have wisdom and love to offer;
remember to provide them with love and respect.

5. A Message for My Sister of Choice

A Message for My Sister of Choice

Our friendship is a sisterhood of sixty plus years
in the making, elementary school through
high school and into adulthood.

We traveled through life's adversities and celebrations,
alone and together, but never lost our connection.
We value loyalty and truth as character traits,
and our ability to work hard/play hard.

We do not argue; we disagree on occasion and agree
to disagree, but we listen to one another,
consider what we hear, and move on.
Distance never plays a factor, and if needed,
we are there, emotionally and physically.

We are trusted confidants that value loyalty.

We are not 'just' friends,
We are sisters of choice who navigate the world together,
and we always return home unscathed.
My sister of choice, I hope you know you know
that you are loved and appreciated.

Dragonfly Message: Life does not offer true friendship
for many.
If you have been granted this gift, please use it wisely
and return the love and loyalty that you receive.
When you have that one person,
don't let that person go - hold tight.

6. Forever - A Mother's Love

Forever -

A Mother's Love

A mother's love, like her children's love, is
unconditional.
Love is filled with great joys, and sometimes great
sorrows.
A mother's love is deep and sacrificial.
It is love that runs deep.

It is courageous, tender, empathetic, celebratory, and
selfless.
Children can see a mother's love as a need to control,
demand or even as interference.
Believe your mom; everything she has done is for you.

This love is support, learned wisdom, and the gift of age.
From whence it comes, a mother's love is full of
extremes.
A mom is loyal and supportive from the moment
she knows you are there.
There is NOTHING you could do that would replace the
love your mother has for you.

She wants all your dreams and desires fulfilled.
She want you to make decisions better than she was able
to do.
A mother, wants everything for her children.
A mother's love, my love, is never-ending,
Always and forever.

Dragonfly Messages: A mother's love is forever.
My own mom passed over two decades ago,
and I miss her.
She put herself in the line of fire to protect her children;
she was fierce. Her soft side loves deeply.
I always return to the childhood memory of her carefully
brushing my long hair. Even now,
I smile knowingly, tthat she watches me.

Don't forget: a mother's love is forever.
Delight in simple memories, or make new ones.

7. The Greatest Gift

The Greatest Gift

Grandchildren...

are God's way of telling parents:
You have done well; your children are striving for and
thriving within a good life.
Parents make mistakes, but look at life's results.

My daughters are strong, empathetic, and kind.
Lissa and Carrie have blessed me with
blended families to love, and learn
from every day.
I am blessed to be the matriarch of this clan,
the Nana, the secret keeper,
and the recipient of so much love.
I am so grateful!

Antonio, Alexis (Lex), Madison (Maddy), Davien,
Jalena, Jason, Aaleyah, and Carmichael,
I love each one of you,
more than you know.
You are the sum of my heart.

It astounds me that these gifts
continue from my grandchildren.

Xavien and Amaria,
you made me a great-grandmother,
a joy many never experience.

If my girls are my soul, then
my grandchildren are my heart.
Grandchildren are the beats that keep me alive.
Family is the riches that sustains me.

Dragonfly message: We are reminded of fleeting life.
Be present, especially with family.
It teaches us more than anyone can imagine.

8. I Used to Be

I Used to Be

I used to be a prisoner, but now I know inaction held me
hostage.
Make choices for you, your needs, not what.
others believe you choose.

"Don't go to college, there's no money for that now.
get married and have kids."
"You chose – no divorce; you made your bed, now lie in
it."

I used to be emotionally barren and physically depleted,
but now I know more, and it will not happen again.
Have the courage of your convictions; be strong.

"You can't afford a lawyer, live with it."
"What did you do to make him mad?"

I used to be afraid, all the time, to live life,
But now I know how to live life to its fullest.
I know just enough fear to delight in life and live on the
edge.
At that time, I was not completely emotionally bankrupt,
Nor was my thinking resuscitated - yet.

"Why can't you live alone? You may marry, again?"
You are making a BIG mistake!"

I used to cry because I existed and felt like a failure,
but now I know I did not exist at all. Happiness evaded
me.
I talked to few, but few really listened, nor did I.

I should have listened to "my gut."
Should have, would have, could have...
But I did not.

I used to believe I was void of dreams, but put on a good
face.
Now I know my dreams and passions were stifled by the
life I was living.
I used to ponder why my life took this turn,

but know I know it was a life lesson.

I used to believe nothing would change, that I would fail
my children,
or that life would get worse.
Now I know, not only did I do my best, but also my
inner-
strength has made me a warrior and a
survivor.

I want to pass on to my children this sense of conviction
and strength.
Let this one realization suffice,
the learning is in the struggle.
YOU are everything and more. YOU are worthy.
YOU are strong survivors.

Dragonfly Message: Change is hard, but it happens.
Don't let others command your life. Stand up,
be heard, and live. Remember, you are worthy..

9. Warrior Women

Warrior Women

Over the years, I've made mistakes.
Omissions of the errors I made, attempted
to shelter you from
life's hardships and adult problems.
It may not have been always
the right decision.

It was always my girls, Lissa & Carrie,
whogave me the courage and strength to fight,
to make hard choices, and to become a warrior.
My love for my girls is the inspiration for
my warrior being and life's passion.
The source of my energy to be better and do better,
grew deep within me.

Now, I am the matriarch, Queen of the clan.

In return, I share with each of you,
my female descendants,
my strength, courage, wisdom, and all my love
for you to protect and pass on to your children.
I am so proud of the warrior women that
exists within my family today.

Dragonfly Message: We should remember
that children learn from what they see, and hear.
Lead your family. Don't be lead by others and send
the wrong messages.
If you slip, get up and be a warrior.

10. A Requiem for Zoey

A Requiem for Zoey

This loving, tiny Yorkie picked me; and
in return I helped her heal from abuse and mistreatment,
and made her family forever.

She came to me around five-years-old,
and it took nearly two years for
her to fully trust me. We became the best of buddies.
On September 15, 2025,
my Zoey crossed the rainbow bridge.
Zoey was a mere 6 weeks from her 15th year of life;
we had a good run.

This tiny, 10-pound dog had the presence of a great dane.

Her teeth were gone and her tongue hung out of the righ
side of her mouth, which caused a comical appearance.
Her Einstein-like hair went every which way when
it was long, and her eyes opened to her soul.

Zoey shared her exuberance for love and life,
until she could not – the morning she passed.

Zoey didn't yap like most little dogs,
but she was my shadow at home,
constantly underfoot; I miss that.
She always conveyed her needswith head nods,
stares, and her gentle pawing if I didn't pay attention.
Zoey sat with me at night, nursed me when sick, and
gave me unconditional love everyday.

We aged together, our hair greying,
our limbs loosing strength,
and losing our sight.
Still we moved forward and with passion.
Our hearts and souls are entangled forever.
Zoey will forever be my fur baby.

Zoey was the ribbon wrapped around my heart.
This deep loss leaves me a bit untethered.
Hher ashes have come home where she belongs,
and she is with me every day.
When it is my time,
Zoey will be frolicking and waiting for me

and we will reunite at the end
of the rainbow bridge.

Dragonfly Message: Zoey is family, my fur baby.
Just like humans we will see them again.
People's beliefs may differ, but hopes
and dreams remain similar.
Grief does not fade, but recesses in our minds,
permitting us to move forward.
The memories stay and make us smile.
Remember to smile.

11. More Than a Storm

More Than a Storm

The robin's-egg blue skies suddenly filled with
clouds of silvery-grey,
and menacing black covers the sky like a shroud.
Humidity rises and the barometer plunges.
Thunder begins to roll meekly across the heavens,
barely a grumble.

The news crawler screams at viewers with distress
"the storm is coming".
Alarms on phones profess the storm's strength and
possible consequences.
Heat lightening flashes all around, and suddenly there is
a boisterous crackle and sizzle as a bolt of
lightning hits the lake.

Rain follows with splats of water hitting the lake,
and the surrounding pavement and buildings.
Suddenly, thunder starts with the brazen force
of a percussion band in a semi-conscientious frenzy.
The rain becomes a deluge.

Intense lightening spreads its tentacles and multiples,
sending sparks and the illusion of fire into the air.
A burst of wayward light energy hits a home here and
there.
The bangs are sonorous as they travel the lake ,
and a few homes go dark.

Meanwhile, all that one can hear is the wind's whisper.
its mournful lament, fighting the instinct to destroy.
It is intimidating.

The deluge of rain, and the faux fireworks continue.
However, the storm retreats as quickly as it attacks.
Lights around the lake flicker on and off,
phones squeal, telling us what we already know –
The storm is over.

For some, this is more than a storm;
it is a reminder of nature's fury.
For others, like me, it is a cleansing,
or a purposeful show of strength
that reminds me that growth can come from
change and discomfort.

This, was a simple storm, quick and biting.
Yet, it cleansed the air,
and produced a calm and quiet night.

Hmm..." she *is* the storm"
really holds pronounced meaning.

Dragonfly Message: Pay homage to nature as she is
strong and unpredictable.

12. Distraction to Destruction: A Dystopian Dream, or is it?

Distraction to Destruction:
A Dystopian Dream, or is it?

The world of my childhood has slipped away.
I fear today's children will forget how to play and
socialize.
The days of red rover, stoplight,
and neighborhood baseball have passed.
Play and creativity replaced by *Mortal Kombat,*
and violence without care.

I fear a dystopian world where no one speaks aloud.
A world where every word is communicated by
technology,
and most of our actions are accomplished by automation.

Is this a world where words and deeds live in the cloud?
Physical movement is silent, or in track-cars and trains
whose echo produces a deafening silence.

Humankind might exists beneath a dome to
avoid the acid rain.
The dome will close quickly if we don't act.
Are we becoming this fabricated world
with a walking dead who lack
empathy or emotions with no need to react?

Put down your cell phones, walk away from
the computers and be present.
Unplug for an hour, a day, a week and remember
the joys, and the sorrows of life.
Take a vacation and enjoy it with those t
people who accompany you.

Talk around the dinner table.
Write a letter or a thank you card.
Go analog for just a moment and breathe.
Return to the real world within which
we reside, and take life in stride.

Laugh and cry, and bring back climbing trees,
and creative play!
Let's clean up this world physically and mentally.
Use technology to our advantage and for good.
If we don't, I worry that humankind will not exist
as we know it in the future.

Take time to see one another,
don't just look, see.
Make the time to connect with another person,
together in the same physical space,
and forge a special bond.

Be brave and stand up against evil residing
in our humanity,
the evil that leaves us barren in numerous ways.
If we as a people do not stand up...

I pray this is no more than a dystopian dream.

Dragonfly Message: Stop and look around at the world.
It is not the world we a grew up in,
but it is the world we know now.
Each person play a part to be kind and caring,

respect technology, and the part it plays in our lives. Think: Is this the world I want to live in or to leave for others?

13. Breakable

Breakable

We begin soft, yet durable.
We experience bumps, bruises, and breaks
of the body and the soul.
We hurt, and we mend.

The more hardened we become,
the more fragile we are.
We remember, we learn, and we grow.

We bend, we we may splinter, but we never shatter.
Our warrior spirit survives as we do.

We still hurt, and we still cry,
Yet, we embrace joy, love, and our own passion for life.
There are no guarantees,
so, we survive embracing what we do have (each other),
and we remain stronger until that momentary lapse,
when we must mend again.

Dragonfly Message: Being broken is something we all experience at differing
levels and times in our lives. Sometimes we need to break to return
to the living. You are strong, you will mend, and you will
move forward and grow.
We need to remember: "sometimes we win, and sometimes we learn". (unknown)

14. Gratitude and Kindness are Foundational

Gratitude and Kindness are Foundational

Life is not the sole act of breathing in and out.
Nor is it just awakening to complete a series of acts
independently.
One must experience what our world has to offer.
Wouldn't it be wonderful if everyone traversed the
World with kindness and gratitude?

Interact with people and animals, they teach us kindness,
But also, teach gratitude with words and acts.
Interactions with others should not be based upon
color, age, gender, race, or ethnicity.
Everyone has something to offer.
Mankind is our humanity.

To be alive is about sharing passion and joy,
and sometimes sorrow and angst.
Sharing these emotions makes each person human.

Embrace others; no one person fully knows another's
story.
It comes back to you ten-fold.
Don't judge. Humanity will be judged.
Stand up and be conscious.
Show your humanity!
Be kind.
Show gratitude, and yes,
continue to breathe in and out.

Dragonfly Message: Kindness and gratitude cost nothing.
Give it freely and often.

15. Food for the Soul and the Stomach

**Food for the Soul
and the Stomach**

Crystal prisms alight the formal dining area
from the sideboards that oppose one another
across the room.
At Christmas, this room is transformed
with a magical feast of foods and sweets.
The room is adorned with crystal chandeliers and crystal
lights that give it a rainbow glow.
Christmas linens cover each sideboard,
are each one is filled with dishes of sour balls
and ribbon candies sugar-coated jelly candies,
fruits, cakes, breads, and of course,
chocolate covered cherries for grandpa.

The smell of spruce and tomato sauce overtakes the

combined smells from the kitchen.
My cousins and I keep walking from room to room
to see what we can snatch before an adult can catch us.
Grampa presides over the living area where
the men gather, andmy Nan rules the kitchen and the
women.
Voices erupt from both rooms,
and raucous laughter fills the house.

Extended family and friends enter the foyer,
each one shaking the snow from their bodies,
and placing coats strewn across the beds.
The bits of light snow and cold fall from
the newly arrived and we are reminded of the nip
in the air and the warm drinks that are created later
tonight.
The women drank tea and coffee
brandy for the men, and hot chocolate with
candy canes for all the kids.
Don't tell grampa, Nana puts a drop
in some of the coffee cups!
Cousins hugged, presents were placed
under the tree upon arrival,
and joy spreads amongst us all.

Once everyone has arrived,
Nana gives the order and plates of food
come rushing by, and end in the formal dining room.
Kids are shooed from underfoot and
gather in the kitchen where a formal
table was set just for them.

Hams, roast beef, turkey, lasagna, antipasto
and more food passes by on Italian ceramic plates.
An army of women returning for mashed potatoes,
vegetables, and dishes of food that I could not name,
but simply knew the food was yummy!

The call to action is sounded...
Time to eat!

The children are fed first, carefully carrying the
'good' plates, and choosing what they
want for this meal.
The children sit and wait, not always with patience,
as the adults fix their plates, and grace
is spoken loudly and after the amen,
a chorus of MANGA explodes
from all the tables. It's Christmas!

The blessings we shared were many on that day.
The lessons we learned were priceless.
Family exists because of love,
friendship, and a need to belong.
Nana fed our stomachs, and Grandpa
fed our souls.
They loved their family and we loved them.

Dragonfly Message: A reminder to all that the elderly
have wisdom,
years of experiences, and lots of love to share.
Do not turn away from them because
they are wrinkled or maybe a bit ill-tempered.
Embrace them and hear their stories.

16. Saltwater Therapy

Saltwater Therapy

The gentle rolls of water create a thunderous crash
as it meets the water's edge.
I am drawn to its beckoning call.

The crunch and crackle of shells beneath my feet are not
a deterrent, in fact, they move me along quickly.
Salt permeates my skin and my other senses,
anda light, white powder dusts my skin and reflects the
light.

The water beckons me to come play, and I do.
Laughter lilts on high and children squeal with delight.
I bob and weave amongst the waves,
and swallow my fair share of sea water.
Pools of seaweed and sticks surround all swimmers,
and tiny fish nibble at one's feet.

After a while, I emerge from the water,
making my way to a blanket in the sand.

Breathing in slowly and releasing my breath,
I return to my patch on the sand where I sit and stare,
and watch others play.
I soak up the sun, knowing this simple act of rinse and
repeat,
will continue to soothe my soul and lift my spirits.
Ahh, saltwater therapy!

Dragonfly Message: Sometimes we need to unplug and
reset.
It is worth your time.

17. A Judge's Signature

A Judge's Signature

Four individuals enter the courtroom
and head toward the judge's chamber.
At age 7 and 11, my sister and I
were dressed by mom for
this auspicious day.
Dress to impress.

We were clothed like twins,
each one wore a gold and black-checkered
dress, complete with a black,
satin sash cinched around the waist.
To complete the outfit our feet shined
with black patent-leather shoes,
and laced, white socks.
We were uncomfortable.

Despite this uncomforting feeling,
it was one o the best days of my life.

We sat in a row, Mom, my sister and I, and Whitey.
The dark, paneled room, without windows,
emitted an eerie atmosphere.
Suddenly, the judge burst forth,
dressed in regular clothes,
not the black robe one sees on the television.

I remember because I was the oldest,
and first to speak to the judge.
I was anxious, but that feeling soon melted away.
The judge was kind and talked to
everyone individually.
Then, the judge addressed
us as a group, and spoke about
changes we were making
and the importance of our choices.

Next, we all signed papers, the judge stamped
everything, and dated it.

43

He stood and said, "Congratulations."
We too, stood to leave.
We walked in four individuals, and walked out a family!

Can I call you dad now?

That was the day I got a dad,
the day that made me feel loved
because my dad chose me.

We arrived home and there were pieces of paper
on the table for each of us.
This yellow notebook paper-strip contained 11 letters
that
heldmy new, last name and my future.
I folded and unfolded that paper all day long.
I held it like a priceless piece of gold that
my life depended upon.
I carried it everywhere until I could spell
my name without looking.

I was so proud!
We were rich now, and not with money.
I had a mom who was happy again, and a dad who
chose me and my sister.
We had a family.

Dragonfly Message: Kudos to the brave individuals who take on another's children with unconditional love with all their hearts, and freely gives of oneself, for they are true heroes.

18. Survivor

Survivor

I am a survivor. I am compelled to be me.
Courage and perseverance put into action,
helped me to become a survivor.
No matter what the catalyst, angst,
depression, inaction letting
go, and not caring about oneself,
requires participation in life.

You know when that feeling of worthlessness
has taken holdof you, and that sinking
into the abyss has you free-falling.
You will know when you have had enough,
and when you ARE enough.
I AM enough, and I am a survivor.

Whatever demons one fights,
they are real and stifling.
Demons visit us all at various times
in our lives.
To become a warrior woman is not easy,
but it can be done.
I am a warrior woman. I am a survivor.

Women put forth a façade, and
others choose not to see it.
If one is lucky, a friend will share truths
with you; if you do not have that friend,
you may mire in the muck a bit longer,
but do not give up.
Think: What is important to **you?**

I worried about my children,
how we would eat, where we would live,
and what am I teaching them?
I worried about the life ahead
and wondered if I could provide
for them and for me.

I stopped worrying and began planning.

I learned to be strong, to be my own person.
I made many mistakes;
and eventually, I learned.
I pulled from the inner strength that I possessed,
and we all possess.
I learned to speak out, to meet my needs and those
of my children.
I would like to believe I was headstrong,
and not aggressive in my stance.

I confronted challenges and fears,
and I sacrificed my own wants for my children.
In the end, my courage and bravery propelled me
to be that warrior, a woman warrior.
I will continue to grow until I am no longer
in this world.
I am a survivor.

Dragonfly Message: Survival, has a different
meaning to each of us. It is completed in
unlike ways. If you are struggling,
know you are strong. Understand that
the learning is in the struggle.
If you have survived in any way,
you are courageous. I applaud you.

19. My Grandparents: Pete & Mary

My Grandparents: Pete & Mary

When the Tea Steeps

Hugs
Smiles
Encouragement
Strength
When the tea steeps.

Learning to believe
In others and oneself
Listening in wonder
Accepting love
Creating a tradition
When the tea steeps.

Nana

Nana was a saucy, sassy woman whose mere presence i
illuminated any room she entered
and always made my grandfather smile.
She never let go of her independence, for her time,
her gypsy-like spiritcould not be controlled; ask
Grandpa.
Nana had been a vaudevillian and could play any
instrument.

Nana turned cartwheels in the backyard with her
grandkids,
and turned heads when she danced
at any social gathering.
Reading tarot cards and foretelling futures
were also part of her repertoire.

Nana was loving and kind to all.
Nana had a way of putting everyone at ease.
And she fed us , spiritually, emotionally, and physically.

Sauce in a big black pot simmered on the stove,
next to a loaf of Italian bread.

Anyone who followed the tomato smell
into the kitchen, acted the thief.
A quick rip of the bread, a simple dip into the pot, and
the culprit would walk away, grinning widely
like the Cheshire Cat, thinking they got
away with the spoils - unnoticed.
Meals fit for royalty decorated the family table daily,
and extra portions existed for visitors
to take something home. Manga!

Roast beef, ham, pork chops, and lots of pasta dishes
filled our bellies.
We cannot forget appetizers, snacks, and desserts,
as well as pasta fagioli and so much more!
She was the glue that held us together.
She was our Dame Mary, our Nana.

Dragonfly Message: The love of grandparents and
their grands is reciprocal.
It builds bonds that help everyone involved
to grow in so many ways.
These connections fills our hearts with love.

20. Laughter

Laughter

Laughter
Loud or soft
A façade

Laughter
Continuous or broken
Protection

Laughter
In the eyes, it dances.
From the mouth, it screams.

Laughter
Verbal tears
A release.

Dragonfly Message: Laughter is an emotion that covers a variety of responses, both positive and negative. We laugh when we are happy or fearful, we laugh when we are nervous, and sometimes we do not know why we laugh. Just remember to laugh.

21. Dragonfly Messages

Dragonfly Messages

The prehistoric-looking nymph flies on high,
with its iridescent wings spread wide.
This intuitive insect glides elusively,
and darts, to and fro.
Dragonflies capture the light in their wings,
only to create a rainbow of beauty and color.

The symbology of this strong and courageous
creature is global.
It is a reminder to live life in the moment
as we are not here for long.
Messages from the spiritual world
are communicated and received in a variety of ways,
to diverse people.
Representative of all seeing and truth,
the dragonfly encourages us to be reflective and

thoughtful, and resilient in life.

Like humans, dragonflies are born of water and
darkness, and emerge into the light to grow and
transform.
I know the dragonfly as I am visited often.
I have learned from their representations, and I know,
I too, will be ever-present when I leave this world,
protecting and encouraging those I love.
The dragonfly is my totem, and I integrate its wisdom
in my life.

Dragonfly love.

www.ingramcontent.com/pod-product-compliance
Lightning Source LLC
Chambersburg PA
CBHW060354050426
42449CB00011B/2977